Quick Start Guide to Easy Online Profits

Chris Lutz

DEDICATION

I dedicate this book to my Mom and Dad for giving me a great start in life.

ACKNOWLEDGMENTS

I'd like to acknowledge all those professionals who were so forthcoming with their knowledge and information to help me along the way.

Quick Start Guide to Easy Online Profits

It's hard isn't it? Knowing just where to begin when you're new to the whole online selling game. With so many others already earning money and touting the praises of their methods, where exactly do *you* begin?

Many "newbies" give up before they've really begun. That's due in part to the unrelenting maze of courses, ebooks, and other assorted sources available as soon as you log in! It's confusing. Who's right? Who's wrong? And who's in it just to make a quick buck from the inexperienced?

Well, hopefully, this guide will point you in the right direction! After all, that **is** the purpose of it :-)

Let's first discuss why people feel compelled to sell products online.

Why To Sell

E-Z Money

Everyone wants to make money. That's a given. And the internet can present some pretty lucrative possibilities. But it can also create a breeding ground for scammers. Sometimes it's tough to know what is a scam and what isn't. No one can tell you in all honesty that they haven't, at some time in their online career, been taken at least once by a hyped up scam. You have to understand that there are some folks who are a constant source of helpful information, and those that are hanging out looking for the quick cash. While you can make some easy profits doing business on the internet, you still must be vigilant and careful when buying. The old adage still rings true, especially online: "Let The Buyer Beware".

Plus, when you sell products online, generally start up costs are much lower than that of a traditional "brick-and-mortar" store. In many cases your monthly costs would be less than going for a night out. So, turning a profit is much, much easier to accomplish.

Setting Your Own Hours

Who doesn't want to be their own boss?! Deciding when and *if* you work gives you such a sense of freedom. Well, not exactly. A common misconception about home-based business is that you will have much more time to do the things you want to, and less time spent working. You see it all the time if you've seen any type of "infomercial" when you're up late watching television. The fact of the matter is any business is still a business.

Meaning, you have to work at it to taste success. Many times, when running your own "stay at home business", there are more work hours put in, and less time for all the fun things that you thought you'd be doing. This is not meant to be discouraging, just a reality check. So be prepared for this ahead of time.

Limitless Opportunity

Earning money online is virtually limitless. Every single day, millions log on in search of something. Whether it be information, or a specific product. Shopping by internet is a time-saver. Collecting information online is a time-saver. Understand that most folks looking for information are prepared to pay for it. This is a fact. And absolutely anything that you can think up can be turned into an informative product. Remember, there are millions of internet visitors all across the world searching for information. The only "limits" involved with selling online are those you set for yourself.

Add to that the fact that with information selling, you can resell the same "packet" of materials over and over again to as many people who want it, and you have an unstoppable income force! However, it's important to remember that technology is an ever expanding field. So you will have to "change with the times" and be prepared to keep your information up to date. Change is a good thing.

Any "idea" can be cultivated into a product. Does it have to be a great idea? No. But, you do need to make sure that you are offering something that has a value. You can't just go and copy down some free information, change some of the wording, and then expect to make a profit. It doesn't work that way. You must put forth effort to get value from what you're creating. This way, if you value and believe in what you have made, then most likely others will too. Plus, eventually, you'll get caught and be labeled a "scammer". And that, my friend, is a reputation you do not want if you want to make your online business a success.

Where To Sell

The first thing you need to do is have a place to sell your products from. It doesn't matter what you're selling, but it does matter where you sell it from. Let me explain. When you plan to run an online business, treat it like one! You'll make much more money this way, believe me. Sure, you'll have some out of pocket expenses, but that's part of doing business. I cannot stress enough the importance of having your very own domain name and web site space.

There's a big difference between a department store and a yard sale. Think of your business as a specialized department store, and give it a place to "stand". If you try and do every single thing for free, you're business will suffer for it in the long run. You need complete control over your business. After all, you are the boss and not just the manager. That's why you need to steer clear of free web hosting sites.

Yeah, they give you your own sub-domain and a

limited amount of space, but more importantly, these hosts hinder your earning ability with permanent banner ad placement and file upload limitations. Keeping everything as simple as possible will benefit you in the end and make your job a lot easier. Don't waste your time or energy. It's not worth it.

So, do yourself a big favor and pay for good web hosting. Let me add this, many web hosts are steering away from allowing certain files to be hosted on their servers. This includes .zip, .mp3, .exe, and in some cases .pdf files. Not good for an information business. Most of these web hosts who ban these types of files are offering "shared" hosting. Shared hosting is simply multiple web sites that share the same server. While this isn't a bad system, it still limits what you can do. But, if you are comfortable with that and have found a shared hosting plan that fits your specific needs with a good price, then go for it. But be sure to check their terms of service before you finalize your choice and pay.

Before you set up with a specific web host, you need a domain name. That is an easy enough task. Where you purchase your domain name is just as important as where you purchase your web space hosting. A good company to go with for domain name purchasing is GoDaddy. They've been around for a while and they have top notch customer service. Plus, their prices are affordable.

When selecting the right domain name it's a good idea for you to add at least one descriptive word pertaining to your online business. Say for instance you want to sell soccer equipment, you might choose

www.waytogoalsoccer.com,
or
www.soccersupplier.com,
or
www.yoursoccersupplies.net,
or
www.justsoccer.com,

The reason for adding "keyword" in your domain is that when people use search engines your site will come up more frequently. And that means more traffic, which means more sales. Plain and simple.

It doesn't matter where you buy your domain name, just that you buy one.

Now, if you're just beginning and don't really have the funds to purchase a domain name and website space, there is another way to begin if you are wishing to sell information products that can be automatically delivered by way of downloading. There is a site that does something quite unique. I know I said earlier that using a sub-domain isn't a good idea for serious online business. But, using a system like TradeBit is the exception to this.

And the reason is quite simple.

First of all, you can get a free 20 MB account, a sub-domain, web based FTP file uploading, built in shopping cart, your own affiliate program, and integrated PayPal/eBay selling plus automated product delivery. This will cut down your work load substantially. Beyond that, they have extensive tutorials in both text and flash that help you "learn the ropes" when using their system.

Besides this, you can always use the redirect function when you purchase your domain name and have a small web hosting space. You won't need a whole bunch of space if you use TradeBit to host your product files. And they allow you to host all the files that shared hosting companies do not. Such as .mp3, .exe, .zip, images and the like. Understand that any files you host you must have the right to sell them. But, if you are a reseller, then this is not a problem.

There is really no good reason why purchasing a domain name and web space should cost you more than $30 realistically. And, if you need more file hosting space, TradeBit offers affordable solutions for this as well that you can upgrade to at any time. All in all, setting up your own online business should cost you no more than $100.

A few more things you will need before you begin are a merchant account, an eBay account if you are interested in selling there, an HTML editor for making changes to pre-designed sales kits or for creating a sales page, and an image editor for creating graphics for your sales pages and products.

There are several different places that you can pick up your own merchant account. PayPal being my top choice due to the fact that it's free. Plus, this is the payment system that TradeBit uses although they are working on adding other systems at the time of this writing. Now, for those that cannot get a PayPal account because of restrictions, you can always get a free merchant account from StormPay. It's basically the same system setup as PayPal. But, you can sign up for a free merchant account on a new system called PayDotCom. They offer PayPal and StormPay integration among others within their system, so it's a good choice. Again, opening a merchant account with PayDotCom is free.

If you have the money and can afford it, there are other merchant account systems out there too. ClickBank being the first on my list. It will cost around $50 to set this up. But don't worry, it's just a one time fee. Also, there is 2CheckOut and they offer a free shopping cart set up service.

Now that you know where you should be selling, it's time to decide on what to sell.

What To Sell

Information Products

This type of selling is probably the easiest way to make fast money without huge overhead costs. And you also have the ability to sell unlimited amounts of information products to as many customers as you can sell them too. But, you must make sure that the information products that you have in stock come with something called Master Resale Rights. **Master Resale Rights** makes it possible within the product terms to resell not only the product itself, but also the right to resell it by those customers you sell it to.

While there are also Standard/Basic/Full Resale Rights, the definition of this is much different. These types of resellable products only give you, the original purchaser of the product, the right to resell it, and not those you sell it to.

Even though Standard/Basic/Full Resale Rights is not a bad thing, having the Master Resale Rights will most certainly bring in more profits based on the fact that your customers can also make money with them as well as learning something at the same time.

With that said, you need to be selective on which resale rights products you buy. What you need to be looking for is a product that is 1. newer, and 2. unique. These criteria usually make for the best sellers. The reason for this is quite simple.

Lots of people jump online searching for an opportunity that will make them some fast cash. The information product business excels in this capacity. That's why so many hop onto the resale rights information selling bandwagon. However, many fail at running a successful information e-business because they have no clue as to what they need to be selling! Or even how to go about selecting a killer product that will generate excellent profits for them without costing them an arm and a leg.

As I said before, you have to be extremely picky. And be wary of "hyped" up sites. Just because the site says that the product is A #1, doesn't mean that it is. There are lots of stinkers out there.

Remember that the owner of the website that is in essence "pushing" a specific product are in the same boat you are. They want to earn money. Things like "I'll be raising the price soon", "Time Sensitive Offer", countdown clocks, and similar are all marketing tactics to get you to purchase right away by creating an urgency. It's a good tactic and it works like you wouldn't believe! But being aware that these are simply techniques will help you in choosing a good product as opposed to one that is unusable.

Along with those urgency techniques, also understand that not everything presented on a "sales page" is what it seems on the surface. Take for instance testimonials. It's important for you to know how some businesses get these and why. First, let's discuss how they get them. A lot of times, authors of products will offer a free copy of their product in exchange for a testimonial. And who wouldn't love something they had to pay nothing for? In some cases, getting that free copy and providing a positive testimonial is a requirement, and not a request. Still yet, other times, the author will ask for feedback to perform final "tweaks" on the product before the official release, and then as a follow up, will ask those that participate for a nice little testimonial to which they offer the participants a "link back" to their own page. It's free publicity. And another darn good way to gain your trust and get you to believe more firmly in the product so that you purchase it.

Furthermore, the reason why those in the online business need these testimonials is to gain your trust in them and their product. Word of mouth carries a lot of weight when it comes to customers purchasing something from you. Again, another marketing tactic that works, and works well.

Always remember that everything you see isn't always so cut-and-dry. There are little things going on "behind the scenes" that you don't know about. Are these things dishonest, maybe. To a certain degree. But there are those that offer testimonials that are completely genuine. Are there sales pages out there that actually speak the truth about the products they are selling? Sure. The unfortunate part is that it's very difficult to know the difference. And the reason for this is that some internet marketers really know what they're doing.

Now, where can you get high quality products for a good deal? One of the best places is through private membership websites. These types of sites are stocked with plenty of resale right information products to get you up and going. Plus, they almost always have quite a number of products that are up to date, or just released recently available for you to download.

Collecting your information products this way will most definitely save you money in the long run.

Add to this the fact that there are products you can actually choose from and decide which you feel are worth selling to your customers. Plus, when you resell these products, which most, if not all, come with resale rights, you stand to make 100% profits from them, excluding selling fees from companies such as PayPal, eBay, etc. I guarantee that having just one high quality resource for your information products, as Allan's is, will bring you a much bigger return on your initial investment of having that membership on a monthly basis when you put your selling skills to work.

There is yet another way to get a decent amount of resellable information products for the cost of but one. You can purchase a "package" of them. Whether this is done by a special sale, or a specific product, you will always get your money's worth if you spend your money in the right places.

With packaged information products, you have to again be very selective. Many resellers the method I like to call "recycling". This is where they will take a bunch of older products and repackage them giving the overall effect of this package being something new. While in essence it is something new, the outer package, what's inside is just the same old stuff.

The best way to avoid buying those information product titles you already have is to read the sales page and look for a list of products included within the package. Most will have this information up there, including an image. If it doesn't, skip it and move on to the next one. If all it has is a title, skip it. You need an honest description of the package so you can determine whether or not you have those exact products already so you're not "double buying".

And to help you out, I want to provide you with a few outstanding titles that won't cost you one red cent. Consider it a gift for purchasing this guide :-) This way, you'll know what to look for by having an example provided to you.

There is one other additional way that can bring you in some pretty outstanding profits. And that is writing up and creating your very own information product. It's really not as difficult as it might sound. And, everyone has a story inside them just itching to get out. Even you!

Physical Products

Of course, you can always sell physical products through the internet too. A great way to begin this is by looking around your own home for items that you want to get rid of and sell them using an auction site such as eBay.

Practically anything can sell and fetch a pretty good price on eBay. In fact, one person was able to sell nothing! Yep, it's an honest to goodness fact. I don't recommend you do that personally as there are plenty of rules you must follow, and doing something like this could get you permanently banned from buying or selling on eBay. So just make sure that you have a product to offer ;-).

Also, when selling a physical product on eBay, you'll want to be sure that your descriptions are accurate. If there's a defect with what you're selling, explain it. Put it out there. This won't necessarily hurt your chances of making a sale, but not adding important information like this can.

Remember too, that since you are selling a physical product, it will need to be shipped out to the individual who bid highest or "bought it now". So, you'll need to add those costs into the price. eBay allows for this, but don't go overboard. Only charge what is necessary to ship the product. Don't be greedy. It will bite you in the end! And having over-excessive shipping charges will sometimes make it harder for you to sell your product. Then you'll be stuck with not only the item you were trying to sell, but also the fees to list it.

It's important to add here that any type of information, or digital product you have, that has the resale rights of course, can be converted into a physical product by placing it on a CD. In fact, eBay encourages you to sell information products in this way.

Now, I'm not going to delve into all the specifics of how to do this as that's not my area of expertise. And really, it goes beyond the scope of this guide. But, I will provide you with some outstanding informative products that will.

Okay, we figured out where to sell our products from, and what we should be selling. So now we need to understand who we should be selling these products to.

Who To Sell To

Knowing who you are selling specific products to is just as important, if not more so, than what you are selling them. How exactly can one find out just who their specific customers are? That's pretty simple. Think about the item you are selling. What is it? Who would be most likely to purchase it? Who would benefit from it? These types of questions can really narrow down your core selling base. And it will help you understand how to advertise your product and get a better response. Understanding your product completely will help you be more successful in the selling process, especially when potential customers have questions that you will need to be able to answer for them.

So, now that you know who you should be selling to, where do you go about finding this select group of individuals? Not too difficult. First off, high traffic sites like eBay for instance, are already comprised of hungry buyers. All they need do is put in a few keywords to search for what they seek and BINGO! There is a nice list provided for them. But be sure that you use as many descriptive words, or keywords, as you can when choosing a listing title for your product.

Say, if you are selling a dvd movie about Dracula. Then you might want to select something like this: Classic Dracula Horror DVD. You get the idea here. People searching for not only a DVD movie, but those searching for the keywords: horror, classic, and Dracula, will also see your listing. Always remember to be honest when you list any product anywhere for sale.

Another great way to find customers that are willing to receive notifications from you about certain products you are selling is by starting up your very own mailing list or newsletter. It's easy to start one, and doesn't take too much time to operate. If you decide just to send previous customers special notices when you have new inventory, that's fine. But be sure that these people want to receive these mailings from you. Otherwise, you're pretty much SPAMMING in their eyes. They have to agree to this type of action. It doesn't matter if they bought something from you. All they agreed to receiving at the time of their purchase was the product they paid for. Nothing more. However, if you approach them in a friendly manner and ask them if they would like to receive future notices about your new products, many times they will agree to that if they are satisfied with your performance.

There are other ways to create your own mailing list though. You can create a sign up form on your web site, use a pop up or pop under from your web site, using free Joint Ventures, or offering free products to those that subscribe.

The bottom line is that previous customers can become repeat customers. And that's what you want!

One last way I'd like to talk about is by getting traffic to your online store or web site. Even if you decide to run a free site, you can still sell products there through the use of banner advertisements, or ad boxes such as those provided by companies like Google. While you may not generate "instant profits" by using this method, you can begin to make a steady trickle of money over time.

We're almost to the home stretch! All we need to do now is focus on the ways in which you can begin selling.

How To Sell

There are plenty of creative ways that you can start marketing your products to potential customers. Of course these aren't all the processes of profit generation, but those listed are some pretty darn good ones. Take some time to read up on each one and try them out. Everyone's path to success is a different one, and yours will be no exception. Most of the methods listed below are more commonly used for selling information products online, but can be adapted to selling physical products also.

Keep in mind, these methods I've outlined for you below are just basic descriptions and there are many different products available that describe each one or a combination of them in lots more detail. Think of this as your "selling dictionary" so that when you begin learning the actual process of selling, you'll know many of the terms that are discussed ahead of time.

The Traffic Method

Using traffic exchange sites is a great way to begin sending floods of visitors to your online store or web site. If people don't know about your business, then how do you expect to make any money from it? That's where these exchanges come in. Although, it's not without plenty of effort and time that will get those visitors to your site. If you want to participate for free, then expect to spend lots of time looking at other participants web sites to earn credits that go towards getting visitors to your own site.

An alternative is to pay for traffic if this is in your budget. Understand though that just because you pay to get the people visiting your site doesn't mean that they buy, or even stay longer than 30 seconds. I would suggest that you try the free traffic generation options available to test the waters. There have been many informative ebooks written on the subject with new ones cropping up all the time due to the popularity of this method.

The Forum Method

This is a pretty simple, but effective method. Forums have long been an incredible source for information. So why not start participating in them? Use a basic search engine and find the right forum that discusses the subject matter that pertain to the products you are intending to sell. Join the forum. Read the posts. Offer your own unique perspective on them. Be helpful. Be friendly.

Everything isn't always about selling, even though this is your main goal. There are plenty of routes to get you where you're headed. It's often said that you must give before you can receive. No truer words were ever spoken. Especially when selling online!

You must be prepared to give something away, even if it's just your own experience, friendly advice, or much needed help by those also participating and accessing the forum. Remember also that there is an existing advertising space already available inside almost every single forum. The signature. This is where you want to place a link to your product, web site, or service with a tiny bit of "mouth-watering" descriptive text. Use that space! It's just as important as participating in the forums. You want to get the word out, so do so in a rather unobtrusive way with the signature tag.

The Blogging Method

Starting your own blog is not only easy, it can also be very therapeutic. And in some cases very lucrative! Many bloggers are making nice profits just from their blogs alone. How can you do this? Simple! Set up a product review section that describes your personal opinions on those products listed, and if you like them, be sure to add an affiliate link to them.

Or you could place banner advertisements on your blog and even charge others for placing their advertisement banners inside your blog. Also, you can add Google box ads inside your blog along the side or even within your posts. You could even have people interested in the information you provide inside your blog pay a monthly fee to access it as a membership. There are plenty of creative ways to profit from your own blog.

The Affiliate Method

By far, this is the most inexpensive and easiest method to use. Every single day people just like you begin earning money from simply signing up for various affiliate programs. It won't cost you a thing past a few minutes to begin earning. That is, you need to become an affiliate before you can see any rewards. Most all affiliate programs will give you all the information and tools you need to begin seeing profits. They want you to succeed.

Otherwise, if you fail, they do too and no money is made for either end. A word of caution though, not all affiliate programs are created equal. Or even close! Some actually pay their affiliates and some, well, beat around the bush and it could take up to 3-6 months to see even one dime from them. Be sure that you read all information available on any affiliate program beforehand. Time is an extremely valuable commodity when doing business online, and you can't afford to waste it on crappy products or programs that bring you zilch results.

The Auction Method

Another popular method for newbies and experienced sellers alike. Explosive sites like eBay have millions of visitors per day, so it's easy to see why this is such a popular choice for selling products online. It can be incredibly easy to list an item for sale and make quick cash when needed with the use of online auctions. However, you must choose your prices, products, and descriptions very carefully to make good profits. This takes time of course to learn the best ways, but it can be well worth it so long as your earnings stay in the "black", or positive numbers.

To sell through an auction site all you need is an account through the site itself, which is normally free, a product, and a payment processor such as PayPal to get your money as fast as possible. And, most big auction sites like eBay offer plenty of useful information along with step-by-step instructions to get you up and "auctioning" quick as a flash.

The "Upsell" Method

Upselling is a tactic in where you offer a product to your customers, they purchase it, and then they are given the choice on whether or not they would like to upgrade their purchase with another product. There are different variations of the upsell and it's purpose is similar to that of the back end method. Take for instance a product that comes in three different version, a lite version(usually something that is free but with limitations put on functionality), a standard version(most commonly with most features enabled within the product but less "comfort creatures" such as 24 hour support, upgrades, etc.), and a pro version(normally this one will have all the "bells and whistles like free lifetime upgrades to the product, a special license to profit from reselling the product, either a resale rights license or an exclusive affiliate program).

Using the lite version of the product, you can give it away as a free gift and then those people you give it to will have the chance to upgrade the product to a less restrictive version. This is upselling in a nutshell. There are plenty of products created out there that use this method to earn more profits.

The Back-End Method

This method is very popular in the ebook information industry. What it does is gives you the power to pull in more profits after you have made the initial sale to your customers by providing you with specific links enabling the reader of the product to buy other related products. Thus creating a built in back-end sales force that runs on autopilot.

Imagine, if you will, having a product that you can not only resell over and over again, but one that has additional purchase links to other associated products within it bringing in more profits to you without you having to do nothing more than distribute the original file.

It's a very easy way to earn extra money after the first sale when you have a good product with a strong back-end. Changing these back-end links to point to your own special affiliate links is also referred to as "rebranding". However, full rebranding gives you special permission and tools to change other important details that help drive traffic to your site by providing you with other rebrandable links and text you can change letting your customers know who has provided this rich resource of information to them, and most importantly, where they can get more!

The "FireSale" Method

I'm sure you have seen this or at least heard of it before. This is when a company or organization has a massive sale at an extremely discounted price to move their merchandise.

Firesales have gained in popularity because of the sheer amount of profits being pulled in from them. It's not unreal to hear people say that they earned thousands of dollars in just 3 days. That's the power of the Firesale. A good Firesale will offer top quality products for an insanely low price, with the price going up by any given percentage or dollar amount throughout the length of the sale. It builds like a fire! Until it's all over and it has burned out, or run it's course.

There are some marketers that sell products online who dismiss these types of sales and never get involved in them. I feel they are doing themselves a great disservice this way. If you can get some great products for an unheard of price, why not? There are specific tools you need to run such a sale, and speaking from experience I have to say that John Delavera has one of the best called JV Manager. It's pricy, but worth every single penny. Of course there are others, but my money is on John all the way.

In addition, you'll need to have your own domain and web space that allows you to upload and access .cgi and, or .php files since many of these types of Firesale programs run on this scripting.

The Membership Method

Creating your own membership site is a very profitable business. It also creates a stable flow of monthly income on a regular basis. That's what makes this method a great one.

Consider this, you could utilize a content management system such as Wordpress and run the whole thing just from it. If you're more inclined to offer a place that is specifically for downloading products like those of the information or ebook nature, then a file hosting system like TradeBit may be the way for you to go. Or, you could even run a membership website from your very own web space with a plugin such as Wishlist Member.

It's not a very difficult method to use, but it is quite time consuming. And there is a lot of stiff competition with this type of site because it is such a successful method. So, you have to think of a way to put a unique spin on whatever it is you are offering. For instance, you could give your members original content, private forums to build a helpful community, video tutorials, etc. This will bump up the value of your membership site over that of your competition. Usually, this method doesn't do that well on auction sites since many of those searching through there are looking for the lowest price they can find.

The "Recycle" Method

Recycling old products for profit is not a new idea. People have been doing this with paper, cans, and other assorted items for years. When you are offering an unused, or used product in your possession for sale, you are recycling it. So it is with information products too. But, there's a difference here.

When you offer a used physical product for sale, you offer it one time, get paid one time, and that's all there is to it. When you sell an resellable information product, you can sell it as many times as you are able to, and can profit with back-end affiliate links or add a free sign up form for your mailing list, generating new leads and more profits over and over again. Now, when an information reseller has products that are a bit older, they will take these and package them up.

In other words, they recycle them and are able to take something that's been on the market for a while, give it a "face lift" with new graphics, new sales copy, and BAM! They have an all new profit generation system. However, they do need to add a few new things within the collection of the recycled products. It makes it much easier to get buyers this way. In my book, Info Product Recycling, this process is clearly explained with more in depth information on adding this method to your selling arsenal.

The Viral Method

Ever heard the saying, "You don't get something for nothing."? Well, this method power-blasts that into dust! Just what is a "viral" product? Think of it as a nasty bug. And this little bug carries itself everywhere until it creates a full blown virus. That's what this method is all about.

You create your own unique product on whatever topic you decide on, add lots of good information and affiliate links inside it, and then give it away. Yes. I said give it away. Everyone likes getting something for free. What makes this method even better than just giving great information away is the fact that you create a product that is chock full of back-end affiliate links for those that receive it from you to change those back-end links so they can profit by giving it away.

So how the heck are you suppose to profit after the downloaders have changed all those links? That's easy! By adding your own advertisements that cannot be changed with your affiliate or direct purchase links throughout it! You could put one or two on every single page or before every chapter of your informative product. Even though all the other back-end affiliate links can be changed, those ads cannot. So you'll still generate profits or mailing list sign ups even though you're giving this specific product away.

Things To Avoid

When starting up any business, there are certain pitfalls you need to steer clear of. That's what this section is all about. So that you can arm yourself with the knowledge of techniques that will lead you down the path to failure. Whether that is time or money losses. Both are important!

I must add here that these things to avoid are things that I have tried myself and haven't brought me any positive results from using them. So you should be cautious before you attempt any of these listed here.

Email Address Buying

I'm sure that you've seen these companies before. Some work, some don't. A majority of them don't. And, unless you can be sure that these email addresses they are giving you are truly double opt in (this is the process of saying "Sure! Send me information" digitally through a doubled process to be certain that those individuals in fact do want the information that's being sent to their email addresses), and not harvested emails (emails that are randomly collected from around the internet with no idea they are being put on lists), it's like taking a shot in the dark.

Anyone can tell a lie. But it takes a great person to tell the truth. Sad to say, there's not a whole lot of those kinds of people doing business on the internet. But, there are still some folks out there you can trust by building a long relationship with them.

I'll tell you this much, the best way to build your mailing list is to do this on your own. This way, you are 100% sure that the email addresses you have and the people behind them really want what you are sending out to them. I would recommend that you think twice, and then think again before purchasing any email addresses from anyone. Especially if the price is cheap.

Safelist Mailing

In a word, NO! Safelists are comprised of others trying to sell their products to each other. It doesn't work. Most of the time, if not all the time, your email ad will go unnoticed and deleted on site. Sure, safelists can be joined for free, but remember, you get what you pay for.

So, if you're paying nothing, expect the same in return. I have personally paid for safelist memberships and have seen an absolute lack of profit return from mailing to them. And the same is true for free safelists. It's a process that's been around for a while, but it simply doesn't work and you'd do well to invest your time in a worthy joint venture give-away instead. At least you'd get something out of it!

SPAMMING

Okay, this one is pretty simple and can be summed up with just one sentence. SPAM is against the law in the U.S. If you're caught doing it, and you will most likely get caught, you will be fined and could have your computer equipment confiscated. There's no reason to SPAM people. It's annoying and doesn't do a thing for you except ruin your reputation.

Time-Wasters

These are a collection of "get rich quick schemes". They are lurking in every corner of the internet. Don't participate in them. Money rotator programs don't work. Pyramid schemes don't work. And the list could go on and on. These are serious time-wasters and will not make you rich. They're crap. Plain and simple. The only real people benefiting from these types of programs are the ones who created the darn things! Think about it. You find this program that sounds pretty good. It only costs you a total of $5.00 to get in. Your member name is put on a list and randomly displayed to get paid for every new member that signs up. But, you only make $2.00. The program creator/operator makes the other $3.00.

And they get paid every single time a new member signs up. You however are put in a pot of countless thousands who's member names get randomly rotated. The owner is sure to get paid, you aren't. Plus, you have to get out there and start recruiting others not even sure that you'll get paid by doing so. See what I'm saying here? It's only quick money for those running the program. Not you.

The "Failure" Factor

This is one of the greatest success crushers there is. And it's all caused by negative thinking and giving up! If you don't have a big following of personal supporters like family and friends, don't worry about it! You won't get anywhere positive if you let the negative comments inside your head. You've got to put those things on the back burner to be successful at selling products online. To heck with the nay-sayers. Are they feeding your family? Are they paying your bills? No. **YOU ARE!**

Every single person has the mental capacity within themselves to be a success at anything they do in life. That includes you. So what if Aunt Sally thinks you're nuts for trying to make money online. Who cares if your brother or sister can't get a grasp on what you're trying to accomplish. What matters is what your goals are and what you believe you can do.

A wonderful saying to remember is: "If you can believe it, You can achieve it!". You *can* do this. It's not brain surgery.

And if your first idea is a total flop, so what?! Get back on that horse and try again. This is where many give up. Not everything you do will be the best course of action. But you will gain the necessary experience through failure so that you can succeed the next time. But you have to give "next time" a chance. Remember, "If at first you don't succeed, try, try again!". If you give yourself enough time to learn and grow your internal knowledge base, you will succeed.

"Too Good To Be True" Products Or Sellers

And finally, always remember, if it seems too good to be true, it probably is. Now, not everything will be a "too good to be true" product or service. There are some people and companies out there that have terrific services and products at unbeatable prices.

Never judge a book by it's cover. Read all the details. Make certain you understand everything in a merchant's terms. If you don't, **ASK QUESTIONS**! Any reliable merchant should be able, and willing, to answer them. If you do ask, and don't hear one single word back, or it takes them an unexplainable amount of time to provide you with the answers you seek, pass that offer over and move on to the next one.

Make Money Online Without Selling Directly to Customers:

If you're the type that prefers to not sell or deal directly so much with customers, perhaps some of the methods below can help you to skim or mine some of the profits from these internet resources.

Make money with your social media accounts. According to Jeff Bullas, "Twitter is a key part of any social media marketing campaign.

However, you don't have to have a blog in order to make money through Twitter.

There are several ways that you can make money through the social network without trying to sell your own products or services.

Twitter is a powerful platform unto itself, not just a conduit for marketing another site. You can create a Twitter account around a profitable niche — making money online, online education, or motherhood, for example — and amass a large number of followers interested in that niche. Then you can tweet links to interesting content from around the web, offering your followers something of value without ever having to create content yourself.

So how do you make money? The same way you do on a blog: Selling advertising, sponsored links, and affiliate marketing. Here are a few programs that can help you make money on Twitter:

#1. Sponsored Tweets
Sponsored Tweets is a well-known ad service for Twitter allows you to set your own price-per-click for ads that you tweet. You can choose the ads you tweet from a list of available ads that are updated regularly. You must have at least 50 followers, 100 tweets, and an account that is at least 60 days old to sign up for this service.

#2. MyLikes
MyLkes is an extensive ad platform can be used on Twitter, Tumblr, YouTube, and your blog. You get to choose ads from thousands of advertisers, and

you get to schedule the time the advertisement will be tweeted from your account. You can earn as much as $0.42 per click, and you can get a payout weekly.

#3. Ad.ly
Ad.ly is another ad service that lets you send out advertisements in your tweets. However, you don't get paid-per-click. Instead, you create a profile of your interests, then advertisers can choose your account to publicize a campaign. You agree to send out a specific number of tweets on a specific schedule, and you get paid a lump sum.

#4. Rev Twt
Rev Twt is a Twitter-based advertising service and is a pay-per-click platform. The more followers you have and the higher reputation you have, the greater access you will have to higher-paying campaigns. Payout is made via Paypal when you have reached $20 in earnings.
#5. Twittad

The Twittad platform claims to be one of the first sponsored-tweet networks. You are able to set your own cost-per-click, but you have to wait for advertisers to accept your bid. You will also have to identify your niche so that advertisers can match their products with you appropriately. Payment is made via Paypal when you have reached $30 in earnings.

There are many other ways you can make money with your Twitter account, including selling banner ads on your profile page, setting your own rates and selling direct sponsored tweets, charging to send a personal message to your followers, or charging for access to your private list of followers. These advertising services can also help you make money through pay-per-click advertising, which can be especially lucrative if you have a large following."

Reference: http://www.jeffbullas.com/2012/05/24/5-ways-to-make-money-with-your-twitter-account/

Auctions

We discussed the auction method above. But, an auction style business or product offering can be relatively hands off. The real work here comes in handling customer questions, and providing feedback on the experience. Possibly even handling returns. If you have good products your customers deem valuable, there should be little of this.

Books

Books, either paperback through self-publishing, or ebooks placed in different marketplaces like Amazon can be easy to manage once created. If you put your book products in these various marketplaces, it really becomes the product of a company like Amazon who is selling it and handles all the fulfillment and shipping while you just collect the royalty. Even if there is a return, they handle it. You rarely engage with the customer unless on the front end through your marketing channels or in person events or relationships. A great resource to use for this is Createspace.com.

DVD's in marketplaces (passively, scaleable)

You can do the same thing with DVD's as you would with books. These can go into various marketplaces also. Or, can be stand alone products even sold through their own sales page through a DVD manufacturer like Kunaki.com. You can publish it, have it manufactured, design your cover and disc, and your price and sales page. There are 2 ways you can make this passive or scalable.

1. Publish at no cost to you with a Kunaki sales page. You set the retail price and we set up a sales page for your product. They accept credit-card orders on your behalf; and manufacture and ship directly to your customers. They provide you with accounting data, customer names and addresses. They send you a monthly check for the quantity sold multiplied by your retail price minus their $1.00 manufacturing cost.

2. Publish at no cost to you with a Kunaki Paypal sales page. You set the retail price and they set up a sales page for your product. The proceeds of each sale flow instantly into your paypal account. Kunaki accepts the order as a pending order. You then periodically pay Kunaki $1.00 plus shipping -- with paypal or credit card -- for pending orders and Kunaki manufactures and ships directly to your customers. You can also prefund your Kunaki account so that these paypal orders are shipped instantly and automatically.

Blog and Articles with Adsense

This was mentioned earlier as well. Here, it is great in that you can produce whatever content your audience is looking for and there's no potentially offputting sales pitches you'd have to make in order to sell your own products. You're simply writing about things you or your audience like and they'll be shown ads relevant to them where you can get paid simply for the ad being displayed to them and more if they click on them. There is the potential for offputting them with too many ads so you want to keep them to a reasonable level and relevant. Google's adsense is probably the easiest resource to use to immediately place on any site to start earning small amounts of money.

You'll need to build lots of traffic over time and generate some clicks in order to make a real appreciable amount. The better your information, and the longer people stay and read, the more that will happen.

Video with Ad Revenue

Here again, this is the same model as with the section above. The easiest and most well-known network for this is Google's Adsense linked up with your Youtube account. When you produce video, you have the option to monetize them with ads by checking a check box. Ads will be displayed to the viewers in a variety of ways.

You can post your videos in other marketplaces that use similar models to multiply your income potential.

Some of the more popular types of videos include:

- Cat videos
- How to and Tutorials
- Consumer Buying Advice/Product Reviews
- Lifestyle

Sell or License Your Pics and Videos Right from Your Phone for Royalties

Clashot is an excellent smart phone app that allows you to take pictures with your phone and upload them to this app which can, in turn, place them in the Deposit Photos marketplace for sale or license. This is one resource, but there are more and more cropping up. Many professional looking and award winning photos have been, and are increasingly being taken by smart phones as the cameras have become so good. Here's something you're already doing anyway and you have the opportunity to make a few bucks from it.

Buy Ads Directly to Affiliate Sites or Links

This can be a rather hands off process once you get it down. Getting your bids for ad actions right first can be a bit of a process though. But, you can easily send bought internet traffic to your site with links, or directly to the product owner's site with your affiliate links and get credit for any sales. There are many products today, especially information products on Clickbank, that offer as much as 50-75% commission on product sales. Some even offer recurring revenue commissions.

Private Label a Product, Have Them Ship to Amazon, Amazon Fulfills.

Fulfillment by Amazon, or FBA, is hot right now. Ideally, you could source a private label product of your own or you can just sell wholesale products (not your own brand). The manufacturer can ship to Amazon on your behalf. The product is sold in the Amazon marketplace. And you collect the money. Amazon takes a share, of course. You tell the manufacturer to ship more to Amazon when the inventory runs low. As with other products in the Amazon marketplace like books, you're collecting the money and profits, but Amazon is handling all the difficult stuff you don't want to do.

Conclusion

In conclusion, selling products online can be an exciting and profitable business. But you have to be very careful with everything you do. Every transaction you make. Every friendship you strike up. Use your common sense. It will carry you far in your quest for internet riches.

My hope for you is that you have come away from this guide and learned more. What you do now with this knowledge is completely up to you. I wish you all the very best life and the internet has to offer, and please, if you need help, use the contact link provided within this product to speak with me.

ABOUT THE AUTHOR

Chris Lutz is the founder and owner of **S.P.A.R.T.A.** With more than a decade of professional experience and a business owner, his business now provides other business owners with tools and resources to run more professional and organized operations.

Chris owns and consults for other businesses in all industries currently and is the author of several other books –

The Entrepreneur Lifestyle
Multiple Streams of Income
Unlimited Customers
Google Adwords Made Easy
Easy eCourse Profits
How to Create a Successful Marketing Plan

His website, www.theentrepreneurlifestyle.com is a celebration of the lifestyle of entrepreneurs and teaches them how to go from struggle to success with tools, eCourses, and other resources for entrepreneurs.

Chris' other website, www.lutzlures.com is an ecommerce site for the outdoor enthusiast and, specifically kayak fishermen.

www.ingramcontent.com/pod-product-compliance
Lightning Source LLC
Chambersburg PA
CBHW071012180526
45168CB00003B/1384